TRANSFER OF QUALITIES

TRANSFER OF QUALITIES

MARTHA RONK

OMNIDAWN PUBLISHING
RICHMOND, CALIFORNIA
2013

Cover art by Farrah Karepetian
Untitled (Broken Jelly Jar, Spacious), 2007
Unique silver gelatin photogram 12.1 x 11.1 x 28.3 cm
From the collection Kristin Rey and Michael Rubel

Book cover and interior design by Cassandra Smith

Offset printed in the United States
by Edwards Brothers Malloy, Ann Arbor, Michigan
on Glatfelter Natures Natural 55# Recycled 30% PCW
Acid Free Archival Quality FSC Certified Paper
with Rainbow FSC Certified Colored End Papers

Cataloguing-in-Publication Data is available from the Library of Congress

Published by Omnidawn Publishing, Richmond, California
www.omnidawn.com   (510) 237-5472   (800) 792-4957
10 9 8 7 6 5 4 3 2 1
ISBN: 978-1-890650-82-7

The liaison that betrays itself by the transfer of qualities...
Henry James, *The Sacred Fount*

1. OBJECTS   11

    VARIOUS OBJECTS   13
    THE BOOK   32
    PHOTOGRAMS   36
    COLLECTING   42

2. PEOPLE   57

    THE UNFAMILIAR   59
    THE FAMILIAR   62
    PORTRAITS   63

3. TRANSFERRED STORIES   67

1.
OBJECTS

For the subject in existence is logically constituted only by the object for which and to which and by which he lives.

Henry James

VARIOUS OBJECTS

The Cup

The cup on the shelf above eyelevel, the reach to get it for the first morning glass of water, the running of the water now clear after the silty water yesterday, the large dragonfly drowning in the cup, now in the bottom of the sink, and the sudden understanding of the whirr that edged the room last night, the unlocatable whirr that stops and starts and finally falls still as the lights are put out and what is left is the neighborhood barking, unidentified sounds pushed to the edge of consciousness, the sudden storm in the middle somewhere, and the knowledge that there must be a reason for what is now silence, a reason lodged in the absent muted clatter, as in the sudden morning appearance of venational wings, each the size of a thumb, folded inside the cup from the top shelf.

The Folded Muslin

Looking at the folded muslin it seemed as if the cloth had extended across the distance to make contact with one's skin—not so much as if one's own gaze had moved out into the world, but rather as if the visible had imposed itself, reached out and seized some part of where you yourself fold, an eyelid wrinkled shut, an elbow creasing. Unable to keep it an object "out there," onto which shape and size and even meaning are imposed, one loses the power to name. It shapes itself to our bodies like the sheets of ghosts or lovers, as when the drape of a storm that has not yet arrived stills the air, puts a slight damp across the brow and under the arms, undoes even the little one knows of science and leaves one utterly enclosed and mute.

The Seashell

The seashell disintegrates into your hand, one now with the palm—slippery, whitened, powdery. With a needle and thread endless hours are spent collecting shells in a bucket, sitting with legs folded under, head bent over, a necklace forming shell by tiny shell. In a 1949 film Olivia De Havilland sits at an embroidery screen poking it again and again with a needle. She thinks of nothing else as the frantic knocking continues at the door.

Lost utterly in the summer heat, untold hours were given over to making these fragile necklaces, to scraping open the small holes that almost always cracked the shell into shards, bits of shell sticking to fingers and skin, falling into the sand and disappearing in the atomized whiteness, only to begin again, to recapture the sense of inarticulate shine that was the needle, the single shell, the blinding reflection off the sand and sea.

A Glass Bowl

You enter the room in which each item has been carefully placed, not perfectly or according to any specific aesthetic rules, but certainly, obsessively. Each has to be where it is, exactly here or exactly there. The verbena sticks up out of its vase just as it should at the far edge of a table bought years ago on a street of junk shops and panhandlers. The blackened Chinese jar arches its handle next to the black arch of a companion bowl, a photographic memory never remembered until intruded upon.

Someone has come in the room and moved the chartreuse glass bowl so chartreuse as to seem a gigantic smudge, and suddenly the room begins to swim. The bowl floats in a wobbly arc into the foreground, the rest of the room dims and you feel suddenly and uneasily intimate with the glassy and sickly surface, glazed over by displacement.

A Glazed Bowl

The hands of those that touched it, the hands that handed it across
the table, over the threshold to you. What absent yet palpable mark
did they make on the object itself, what quality now removed,
slipping out from under the glass glaze, out from Faenza, out from
the Italian streets and Madonna of the Graces and into the air—so
that although the bowl remains as "useful" as before, it is no longer
a prop for what went on in the awful heat wave that consumed the
day we stood in the shop handing the small objects back and forth
between us or the role it played at the dinner when there were eight
of us, glasses flung to the street to celebrate the New Year, a small
piece of the theater on which the curtain is now drawn.

A Lecture

Presented to us, it was so fully rounded and incised that it could be passed from one person to another as one might pass a Craftsman vase, deeply and opaquely green. It was not only that the words were equal to the subject matter, but also that there was something formally complete so that one could take hold of the ineffable and turn it about to examine it from all sides, could reach into its center as if into the center of a vase so that, surrounded by the rounded surfaces and as if oneself had emptied out the clay to produce this pocket of air in which to situate oneself, one could utter a tone that would echo off the sides and circulate as a thought through the entire hall in which we all sat as still as objects lined up against the wall.

A Paper Crown

You realize some piece of you has to be pierced in order for the almost unbearable desire to be slotted into place. Do you suppose they do that anymore, cut slots in cardboard for paper tabs, the small hats fitted around the heads of small children waiting in line for the play to begin, their lines circling their brains so they won't forget, "I'm coming my prince, my princess, I won't forget you, I won't ever forget you," and when the performance, and the school, and the brick, and the street are memories that come only in fits, the way crayon skips on the grainy surface of the paper you've folded up for the crown, you realize what the embrace of what you thought you could die for has cost you.

A Lost Thing

You hate yourself when the object that defines you, or at least you think it does, is lost or broken. It makes perfect sense: you are the one who is lost and it's your own fault, having left it behind in a stranger's room for where else but in the room of a stranger would you leave it, inadvertent, shoddily careless, the enemy of attachments. Or it is that you run through the room in a hurry—*slow down* you hear someone say—rushing out the door, knocking it into a thousand pieces, glass shattered on the floor, the frame twisted, a strange disfiguration replacing the face—the photographic paper marred by shards—and it's not only the having done it that one must live with—one's own arm thrown carelessly through the air— but the evidence of what was meant to be.

Clothes in the Closet

Limp as dishcloths, they hang, useless in the backs of closets—
jackets or dresses or shifts worn in years gone by. You might, you
once thought, wear them again: that fashion might return, you
might gain or lose weight, feel as swaggering or slightly demure.
Lift shoulders, cross legs. You might try on the past as costume just
to look in the mirror to see who it was who wore it. Some have
disappeared in boxes to Goodwill. Some have been turned into rags.
But some are draped in plastic and hang there year after year. They
evoke extraordinary days—occasions for velvet or brocade. For a
while there are the usual illusions of return, but ultimately, they are
painful reminders that they won't ever fit, not so much because of
the body's vagaries, but because even parody is impotent against the
time that time has become.

Corroded Metal

What I found was a flat piece of metal, corroded, pocked, and shaped quite like a cloud. I hung it over the sink in lieu of a window and looked at it. We wonder what, if anything, objects want, if our rearranging satisfies some hidden need not only of ours but of theirs. Things found in the gutter and rescued, we say, are given another life, but as what—to be looked it, handled, to be made into what one wills, as if one were still a child and had no sense of the so-called value of a thing, but could find in a coil of wire, a bit of cardboard, a flat piece of metal all the possible worlds one might want, given time enough to conjure. So perhaps it is this— this time of seeming eternity that objects want and have no way of requesting, just as we have no way of guaranteeing either for them or for ourselves.

The Contest

I remember the woolen area rug as it curled at the ends and provided
the exact obstacle to walking, perfect for tripping and she was so
very old at the time that everyone in the family thought it, although
brought all the way from Russia, woven by small fingers, should,
although she wouldn't hear of it, be removed. Red and faded, the
Kazak lay at the foot of the stairs, a bold medallion design, 49
knots/sq. inch, lying as if in wait. Her translucent hands moved
on the white sheets sliding over the selvage and refusing. Slippage,
hip bones, fibula, tibia, cuneiform. It is disturbing even in memory,
pressing hard up against balance and composure, the reoccurring
and unevenly matched contest with things.

The Window

The window is both a thing in itself and a transparency that obliterates itself by being itself. The thing itself is the wooden frame and cross pieces, the smudged glass panes. The frame creates both an exact view—a tree cut off at the right edge, a corner of roof and jacaranda blooms—and also a frameless view that pulls one off the seat one is sitting in, towards the walls on the other side of the room and out into the blinding white of the morning. It is between inside and outside, between every picture one has seen of trees and these trees, between stasis and movement, between the certainty of the keyboard beneath the fingers and possibility, both the slight noise of tapping and the tapping of branches on the window, creating an illusion, belied by the weighty body, of a weightless glide into the California light that seems the absence of all light, transparency itself.

A Prop

One is no longer fully present. Now, all experiences seem set in a context so large and increasingly complex, that one is more than distracted, almost obliterated by all else that is going on and indeed all that will be going on after one ceases to be. For it is this sense of one's own absence that makes it impossible to respond fully and with the sort of ticklish anxiety with which one used to respond— not a full fledged anything exactly, but edgy and on guard, as if the foil were about to be thrust in one's direction despite having chosen a corner at quite a distance from the main stage.

I've been in constant practice, Hamlet says to Horatio, and so is ready to stand in front of the other almost identical young man and exchange parries. In the theater it is almost possible to grasp an épée one has never held, to remember a time of being fully present.

Branches

Is intimacy held tight in the gesture, the gap in the sky where branches cross, the crossing of branches, the small unholy sticks? Of course at the window, of course at the window at night. The small gesture, lifting as he lifts his finger. The sharp way you feel the lift, as if jabbed in the chest. In the photograph of Ansley Park, 1992, the zigzag pattern across the ground, the one leafless twig glowing in the black half, the other darkly outlined in the white half, the way we are marked by our gestures, your swimming ones in and out of your body, towards and away, the precision of them, the angle of branch, how you opened up the sky, how I was marked by it as the photographic paper by lines of black and the gap where they are missing.

A Postcard

Is there any way to understand why one had to buy it in the first place, or why one clings to the fleamarket postcard in the basket on the bookcase? She's not around. The card would exactly suit the person whose immediate presence is missed. I hold it in my hand, could send it through the mail, and imagine it in her hand in some other place—but this one that could originally have been mailed for 2 cents, isn't the one I send, this one with a picture of a two story house, bare trees and snow is one I pass over every time I thumb through the collection since it should be sent from the heart of the country to me to remind me of railroad tracks and depression era glass from a missing visit to a missing relative if I had been such a person.

A Photo of a Junk Store

If the photograph itself is of objects, objects, for example, in a shop window, to what extent is the photograph as object put in abeyance as if one were looking at the various metal devices and scientific equipment directly—or as directly as possible given the smeary and reflective surface of the plate glass window itself. It's hard to make out exactly what is in the window although it is also hard not to want to penetrate to the core. Yet once having penetrated, the things disclose their potential for harm, as if one had banged up against them even to the point of injury, as if one's own memory were full of furniture with sharp edges or stuffed manikin replicas of one's own body the color of hospital stockings pulled over one's face like the mask of a robber threatening the shop clerk within.

A Photographic Album

One of the photographs is missing, just remnants of glue and small black wedges that held it so long in place. The photograph held a scene long gone, both now missing as is the experience of this tiny realm of experience, of turning the pages of a photographic album as the relatives in my family used to do through long winter afternoons as if there were no hurry at all, commenting on the old Buick, although not in recent years since most of them are dead or live so far away that, although they may still be doing such things, turning pages slowly as the couch sinks into collapsing springs, I no longer am witness. And the turning of any pages at all, they say, just a matter of time.

Lost Things

There was a photograph at the antique book fair, a cyanotype of a solitary Indian canoe and once I had seen it, I had to have it. Something seemed to be moving into this blue scene of boat and water like fog out of the past. It covered my skin in a scrim of cold and clenched my teeth until my jaws ached and I kept staring at it as I had stared at certain images when I was a child, as if I could hear words of the sibyl from some crevice, as if something—although it never was—were to be made manifest. The invocation of one object by another appears both obvious, yet also random, dependent on idiosyncratic infusions of one's own.

Years earlier I had been given a painting of a blue boat by a young love who later committed suicide. The painting itself was lost in packing up or left with someone to retrieve later or—I can't even remember where I last saw it, and can't say what I could have done with it or how I felt when the sudden image invaded me through the cyanotype by Edward Curtis. I never thought the chance finding of the blue canoe would alter my own guilt and grief, but the fact that it was an actual object, not just a memory, created the illusion that things have a tropic power unregulated by time and space.

One dies at the thought that any object to which one is attached is lost, and in this mortal fear one also feels that this object is nothing, an interchangeable sign, an empty occasion.
   Maurice Blanchot

Equivalents

In April of 1905 Henry James met with Alvin Langdon Coburn to create the photogravure frontispieces for James's New York Edition. Directed by James, Coburn was to search out visual equivalents of things or places that were linked to the text in some tangential and symbolic way.

James and Coburn were looking for an *"aspect of things or the combination of objects that might, by a latent virtue in it, speak for its connection with something in the book, and yet at the same time speak enough for its odd or interesting self."*
James to Coburn, 26 June 1906, James Collection, Virginia.

What this collaboration manifests besides the provocative juxtapositions of text and images, is a sense, articulated by Henry James over and over in the prefaces, that objects have a meaning of their own that they "give out" if only there are those present to receive.

To be at all critically, or as we have been fond of calling it, analytically, minded—over and beyond an inherent love of the general many colored pictures of things—is to be subject to the superstition that objects and places, coherently grouped, disposed for human use and addressed to it, must have a sense of their own, a mystic meaning proper to themselves to give out: to give out, that is, to the participant at once so interested and detailed as to be moved to a report of the matter.
Henry James, *The American Scene*

THE BOOK

So much for statues and vases. I hope books are not like them. Buy a vase, take it home, put it on your table or your mantel, and, after a while, it will allow itself to be made a part of your household. But it will be no less a vase, for that.

On the other hand, take a book, and you will find it offering, opening itself. It is this openness of the book which I find so moving. A book is not shut in by its contours, is not walled up as in a fortress. It asks nothing better than to exist outside itself, or to let you exist in it.

In short, the extraordinary fact in the case of a book is the falling away of the barriers between you and it. You are inside it; it is inside you; there is no longer either outside or inside.

George Poulet, Criticism and the Experience of Interiority

1.

The word in the sentence has been smudged, the ink blotted, the paper overfolded, the meaning derailed; the sentence now pale, missing its force and import, languishing as the characters in *La Bohème*, sickly as music without words. The others, the ones intact, try to make up for the missing word and proliferate a range of meanings consistent with the vocabulary and syntax, yet still it is the realm of guesses, guesses as to the missing, as to the alteration in meaning, as to the endless possibilities contained in what would otherwise have been a quite mundane sentence leading to the next in the paragraph, but which now has taken over completely given the aggressive force of the uninvited guest.

2.

For a writer, the intimacy of the image is in submitting completely to what one has imagined and put on the page, to oneself one might say and yet not oneself, an onanism without guilt, the subsuming embrace of an image abstract enough as not to flush the skin, yet vivid enough to cause a collapse into the lilies as if trying to remember the names of the angels and archangels and all the company of heaven, although one never can, just the overwhelming smell of them at the side of the greenhouse door—so much white odor, dusty stamens, the moment of her modest rapture as she saw him appear in the archway with the single flower, the ceiling a complex mosaic of blue and stars, *ave gratia plena dominus tecum.*

3.

The book lies open and prone but keeps closing itself like an irritating fan if the body beneath shifts position from side to side. The paper is there; the fingers are there, and they slip in and out of one another. Yet immersion in one of these things is not, one first thinks, an encounter with the material and restless thing on one's lap. It is rather an encounter with a tyranny of sorts, a haunting into the next hours as a character whom one has never met comes closer, not inhabiting exactly, not taking over thoughts and gestures, but warmer than a fictional character ought to be, standing too close and breathing hard in an internal landscape that was once your own and through which you are both walking where the fictional snow is a kind of snow closer to paper confetti than rain, its texture not unlike the feel of the page underneath your fingers.

4.

No one else seems to catch the overwhelming odor of mold that creeps along the floor, that intrudes in random moments as one's attention is focused on a passage in a book one has been meaning to read for weeks. In the story, there are many scenes unfolding, rubbing up against one another like that dirty yellow fog against the window pane with which we are all so familiar, and in such a way that it is impossible to isolate one discrete moment from any other in order to understand it more thoroughly or to penetrate more deeply. Rather, there is a sense of increasing distraction such that one must attend with all one's faculties lest one miss even an iota of the characters' accumulating shame. Yet, of course, despite one's efforts to lose oneself in reading, the odor is throughout the room and onto one's skin and has affected proportionally one's disgust at the emanations from the page.

5.

What one is seeking is the loss of oneself, not in the sense of terror or anxious concern, but in the sense of being seized out of oneself and able thereby to see or hear most profoundly as with obliterated eyes and ears; and it is often by the juxtaposition in writing of the abstract with the specific that such seizure occurs. The friction between two unrelated planes—one entirely vaporous and one sharply delineated—seems by *discordia concors* able to blot out the regular senses. No matter if the image seems exactly fitting or to come astonishingly out of nowhere, it wrests one; and for one split second, it is what is, and any trajectory forward is halted and one locates one's absence with erotic relief.

> Our two souls therefore, which are one,
>   Though I must go, endure not yet
> A breach, but an expansion,
>   Like gold to airy thinness beat.
>   John Donne, "A Valediction: Forbidding Mourning"

6.

It is useful to sit on if you're small; the side to side squirm on top of a large-sized book slides into one's adult mind. Someone says to put a dictionary under foot while working at the computer. It is useless for looking up words—the print is miniscule, the online OED more efficient. Oversized have a special roped off section in the library stacks; they are heavy to lift, to take home, to use. Often beautiful, with drawings of orioles and beetles, camellias and vein lines, these oversized are also awkward to hold. Their spread requires the expanse of a library table. Across this surface into the feathers of the Audubon wingspread and into the damp but preternaturally extended afternoon—it seems to go on and on—the winged power of uselessness.

7.

Hamlet refers to "the book and volume of my brain," and with the one word, "volume," points simultaneously to books as volumes of written words and to the volumes of space inside the globe of his skull. The oscillation of the two meanings, between the "book" as mentally conceived and the book as an object to be picked up and held, a thing to be read, the volume Ophelia, as directed by her father—"Read on this book, that show of such an exercise may colour your loneliness"—lures him with, makes a reader of the play helplessly intimate with this character who is as mere words as unreal as the clouds he sees as camels or at least says he sees, an insubstantial pageant.

Thus there is in the life of a collector a dialectical tension between the poles of disorder and order. Naturally, his existence is tied to many other things as well: to a very mysterious relationship to ownership... also, to a relationship to objects which does not emphasize their functional, utilitarian value—that is, their usefulness—but studies and loves them as the scene, the stage, of their fate.
Walter Benjamin, "Unpacking My Library"

PHOTOGRAMS

The fact that the object touches the photographic paper during exposure to light, but is gone once the image is made reveals an essential characteristic of the photogram—an absence is felt as a presence.

The object—a paperclip, a pair of scissors, a plant stem—seems to have moved into a realm between itself and the paper. It is eerily both a tangible thing and an image; it suggests the graspable and mere graphic shape. "Reality" moves closer, impinges strangely.

Writing about the transfer of qualities between objects and people also works a kind of exchange as if the paper on which the words appear were like photographic paper, and as if the form of the prose poem dissolved more boundaries than between prose and poetry.

Man Ray called his photograms "Rayographs," combining his name and the source of light, and he likened these to André Breton's "automatic writing."

For photography is an imprint or transfer of the real; it is a photochemically processed trace causally connected to that thing in the world to which it refers in a manner parallel to that of fingerprints or footprints or the rings of water that cold glasses leave on tables.
　　　Rosalind Krauss

Man Ray has quite ordinary, everyday objects, pop up in his Champs Délicieux.
They hover around there like suddenly freed, living beings that had been shut up
for ages and, unobserved in the shelter of darkness, were taking their first steps
in the cosmos.

Experimental Vision: The Evolution of the Photogram since 1919

1.

The paperclip is of a size to be picked up between finger and thumb
and dropped into the paperclip jar on the desk. True to form and
exact. The object reproduced is the same as the object itself—the
human element removed to intensify the illusion of reality—as if
the thingness of the object were its only and most palpable point.
Despite current ways of seeing in which we all adjust for size, the
photogram demands the setting aside of such faculties to acquire
new ones. The paperclip, the safety pin, the leaf specimen demand a
far more rigorous discipline, the discipline of taking things exactly
as they are.

2.

Pliers and wire, the V of the pliers as heavy-handed as an autocratic
command, as vicious, as weighty in the hand as certainty. The
skin turns cool from the metal, smells of metallic ozone, shifts in
tactile weight from one hand to the other. The tight grip of the V
is outside the zone of flutter—one's hands fluttering in the face of
the precipitous dream-fall endlessly spiraling through uninhabited
space. But it's day. Things need be done. The wire requires the proper
tool. Certitude is the object captured by the object that holds things
in place.

3.

A spoon darkened in heavy outline, a splay of mesh letting in dashes of light, and whatever is egg-shaped, balanced as if in a foot race against time. The curdling of eggs, the decay of monuments, the light dusting of lines across her brow. The teetering balance of a spoon in one's hands, across the thumb, the outline of seductive fingers captured in mesh gloves. *Spon* from the Anglo-Saxon, a shard of wood. Another definition: lying together in a curved form. Objects just lying around.

4.

L'objet entre le papier sensible et la source lumineuse—and so the open scissors rest on the paper itself and the object is captured—a tactile process that exaggerates the illusion of presence. Your hand makes the shape of a scissors in a child's game. The shadow of your hand against the sun-lit wall makes the clicking noise of rusty scissors. A sort of laying on of hands on the document—so often just the imposition of an opened hand, the movement of mortality in the scissored fingers, cartilage so thin as to be transparent. Each leaves a hand print for a future. Unseen, the life blood is draining day by day.

5.

Against deep black the crook of the eyeglasses sweeps a hand behind an ear and the smooth C of skin between the ear and the hairline. The arc of the gesture in the shape of the eyeglass stems. The object links directly to the other objects of one's body that are objects in themselves and the glass itself is the glasses of the eyes, where when I looked into them after his accident were dull metal—so lacking in light I had to believe in the intangible soul that had, I couldn't help but think, left the body an empty husk, the soul off on its purgatorial wanderings, so that damaged by contagion I could no longer look directly into anyone's eyes.

6.

The life of a shadow is all movement and light or all absence of light as the wing eclipses the sunlight or as light itself flickers across the paper, inscribing an illusion of birds falling through air. As roller pigeons somersaulted, they made circles over the house, as if they would plummet to earth and we held our breath as they hurled themselves "hither and thither." An old fashioned expression harkening back to *The Canterbury Tales* and *Piers Plowman*, "hider" rhyming with "slider," lines of light sliding across the sky by chance, and by chance evoking the opposite: birds got hold of, bird feathers throbbing hot in one's hands.

7.

That objects have shadows, that the intangible shadows impress upon us the solidity of the object. That what is entirely objective is bafflingly abstract. That the object touching the paper during exposure is gone in the image. That a mechanical process should express for us not only affection for an object, but actual intimacy, the skins of separation somehow dissolved. A longing to be touched, disintegration of fixed systems, an erasure of gender. A skin of emulsion coating the pores, oil rubbed over all the parts, a gratuitous act terminating in gift.

All of these pictures are like shadows or imprints of objects, which is part of the play on the idea of the ghost...the idea of the shadow or negative image. I was interested in capturing a form which is departing, like ascending birds or smoke
Adam Fuss on My Ghost

8.

Shadows extend across a slope of lawn late summer. The shadow of a hand falls across the open book. The shadows are captured by the flash of light on the light-sensitive paper. Then a bird, then a cloud.

The shadow of what is over, day 8, a loop between what was and what will be, sitting in a peeling lawn chair in the waist of the 8, never going backward, never going forward, as this moment slides towards the lower part of the lawn unnoticed. How the shadows move in and when the sun hits the yellow burst of leaves, how they are quelled for the half hour before it is decidedly twilight and almost opaque, and it is there one finds the words one's been looking for, previously hidden, now suddenly set free.

Laura Mundy, December 12, 1834 sends in response to the package of beautiful shadows, a photogenic drawing of leaves and coiled tendrils. In 1833 Henry Fox Talbot imagines natural images imprinting themselves durably, remaining fixed upon the paper. A negative contact print of a botanical specimen is dated circa 1835.

9.

Petals made limp by rain on the bodies of daylilies, a strip of collapsed flesh across the palm. Each day numbers of them are *over*, needing to be deadheaded, hung over as after an evening of ruinous gin. The rayograph flower blazes white out of the past as corsages on black dresses in an era of the surreal—whiter than any flower out of the ground, this one blossoms out of paper exposed to light and persuades that radiance lasts, 11x9, 1925.

What does the line mean, "that's got his own, that's got his own," what child would that be, what did she mean with her white gardenia in her singed hair? The first time it was in the midst of gin, the singer who sang it with gin in her veins.

10.

Melted glass bottles recycled as images of melted glass, the capture of melt in iconic form, a form of metamorphosis, of this leading to that: the conversation that, having faded, erupts in a brilliant cluster, the ruination that sneaks out the back and speeds off down the open highway. Ruin as an idea of possibility, the outcropping of moss, the proliferation of lichen—miniature islands on stone— craggy prospects and yawning gloom. Ruins show us a world in which beauty or sublimity is sealed off: it is a melancholy world in which no recollection is possible; eternity appears, not as such, but diffracted through the most perishable.

The jug's jug-character consists in the poured gift of the pouring out. Even the empty jug retains its nature by virtue of the poured gift, even though the empty jug does not admit of a giving out. But this nonadmission belongs to the jug and to it alone. A scythe, by contrast, or a hammer is incapable of a nonadmission of this giving.

Martin Heidegger, *Poetry, Language, Thought*

COLLECTING

Fragility

The yearning for fragility: breakable bowls, plates, pitchers, and vases. If a piece is old and if it has been broken and mended, its fragility exposed by means of glue and cracks, it seems even more profoundly touched by the sensual and uncanny. More forbidden and more transparently on display—as objects behind store windows, as an insect caught in see-through amber. The strange trance that attaches to finding a Chinese pot with small useless handles or a bowl the color of a lunar moth seems to indicate that such objects are replacements, as Freud suggests, for something repressed. One's history masquerading as an object. If the object is also transparent, it is tempting to stare, imagining that one could strain one's eyes to see the effects of time deep within.

If the piece comes not only with cracks but with dirt from the ground out of which it was dug or from years on the back shelves of a junk store—as the plate painted with green cherries found in Faison—how did it come to be there by chance just when I also was there? How did it survive all the careless sinks and hands, earthquakes and upheavals?

When I manage to get it home wrapped in layers of newspaper, its fragility fills me with an almost painful and heightened attentiveness. I want to peer into all the potential ruin it contains, its evocation of a melancholy both addictive and irritable as is Jacques's in *As You Like It: And so, from hour to hour, we ripe and ripe, / And then, from hour to hour, we rot and rot; / And thereby hangs a tale*.

Fragility opens all to vanishing, a fragility that doubles one's view of an object, as if "shattering" appeared in mid-air overlaying the thing itself, somersaulting along with the fluttering and moth-like blue.

No recollection is possible any more, save by way of perdition; eternity appears, not as such, but diffracted through the most perishable.
      Adorno

Arrangements #1

Changing things in a room is what to do when everything is wrong with everything; an excess of loathing lifts couches and chairs and lamps until it settles, until the next time. The side table begins to make a sort of inauspicious commotion; to get it to stop, it must decidedly be shifted. Each arrangement of objects suggests a rearrangement of ideas or words or at least a platform from which to begin. As if it were possible to change one's psychological configuration.

Marianne Moore revised "Poetry" from many lines and details down to three, keeping her sense that poetry should contain "the genuine." Ezra Pound revised "A Station in the Metro" down from several paragraphs to a haiku with gaps between words. Perhaps the room should be stripped, taken down to bare walls and a few sticks of furniture as if you'd just moved in. One might wish for such austerity, such clarity, some sense that underneath were some authentic core rather than, as seems most true, that it is spread out all over the room, out the door, into the air and into the water supply spreading cholera in Haiti.

I spend several hours a day sitting at my work-table. Sometimes I would like it to be as empty as possible. But most often, I prefer it to be cluttered, almost to excess. The table itself is made from a sheet of glass 1 metre 40 in length and 70 centimetres across, resting on metal trestles. Its stability is far from perfect and it's no bad thing in actual fact that it should be heavily loaded or even overloaded; the weight of the objects it supports helps to keep it steady.

Georges Perec, *Species of Spaces and Other Pieces*

Arrangements #2

In the midst of shifting things in the room about, something happens. Somehow and for some reason—the result of pain or grief or loss or for no reason you can locate—a sort of blankness has taken over. You yourself are rearranged and no longer care about how things are put, whether this is here or there and whether someone will notice. Whether you wash your hair, whether you show up. Of course efforts are made to keep things going in some recognizable way, but indifference has covered all the furniture like swaths of cloth once thrown over the couches and chairs when a family decamped. The shapes are vague, bulky, dead as corpses in their winding sheets.

The qualities that used to define objects now define you. Even as they often seem to be in unexpressed mourning for voice or dance (as in the stories of dolls up and about in the dead of night) so too are you. The threads that once connected you to others are frayed and you can't seem to care. Most debilitating and shameful, this state affects not only insignificant matters but deep moral judgments as if they were connected by the practice of attention itself. Have you turned into a person so shut down that you're a mere thing among things? A body no longer a body for use, but a container in which some non-existent insistence has taken up residence and colonized the whole. Unable to negate this alien thing, you turn this negation against the things of the world.

At the museum I return to the rooms of Cycladic art (2800–2300 BC), but this time the folded arms of the statues are not an archeological puzzle. The women with their clitoral slits and incised arms are withdrawn into themselves, pulled back from a world that comes at them; they are isolated, wrapped round with their arms, unknowable, lost to time. Early figures are shaped like violins. Each figure is the embodiment of immobility. You wonder about their closed-off quality—you think of certain practices that might foster such remove—and what such remove means. You look in the vitrines at the stone women and wonder not only about the abstract objects themselves, but also about those who made them. What were these female figures for? What did they see in these object-like creatures so tightly self-enclosed and self-protective, so obsessively bound up in themselves and removed from everything around them? Why have they been arranged in a way suggesting an emblem of loss itself or have you come to see the world from inside your own folded arms, your own vitrine?

Talking to Things

Nothing has an essence of its own, but is what it is only in relation to all that is around. This awareness is often unconscious, sometimes highly philosophical and sophisticated, liberating or embarrassing. Each shift, each bend of one's body, turns out to be related to the potency of objects. Sometimes, objects create violent disturbances, especially those occurring by "chance": the signet ring stamping a death decree for Hamlet, the manuscript lost by Ejlert Løvborg in *Hedda Gabler*, the will that hounds Richard Carstone to distraction in *Bleak House*, the golden bowl in Henry James.

We talk all the time to the things around us, computers of course, but also cars, shoes that rub, spatulas that slip, and, and as children, toys. We yell, swear, throw them on the floor. We appeal—as it is often difficult to appeal to a person—to a mirror, a candle, a photograph, a shot glass of whiskey, or, if devout, a holy book. For Baudelaire this is the beginning of melancholy:

The overriding desire of most children is to get at and see the soul of their toys, some at the end of a certain period of use, others straightaway. It is on the more or less swift invasion of this desire that depends the length of life of a toy. …When this desire has implanted itself in the child's cerebral marrow, it fills his fingers and nails with an extraordinary agility and strength. The child twists and turns his toy, scratches it, shakes it, bumps it against the walls, throws it on the ground. The child makes a supreme effort; at last he opens it up, he is the stronger. But where is the soul? This is the beginning of melancholy and gloom.
    "A Philosophy of Toys"

Objects are ever silent, but there may be, nevertheless, responses of a sort that shift things as if cells had been rearranged. In some ways objects, alien and self-possessed, so resistant to interpretation, speak of an acceptance of the way things are.

Often there's a pervasive and quiet exchange between oneself and a thing, an interdependence more akin to a complicated and subterranean conversation of adjustments and reconsiderations, a way of negotiating one's way through the world without words, only gesture—sliding between chair and chair, lifting an arm to put the glass on a shelf, sweeping a hanger across the pole in the closet. In some ways objects "speak" directly to the body and alter a route through the room creating slight vectors of pressure. The drawing I'd make of it shows thin ink lines from each object in the room to each other object, door, person, rug, crayon, phone, paper bag, plant—until the page is crisscrossed with lines.

In some ways, perhaps most significantly for a writer, objects generate trains of associations, images, memories, whole narratives. As things pass from generation to generation, from this person's hand to that, they accumulate history and a ring becomes haloed with an aura of its entire past. Famously, things spur the memory: Proust describes stumbling against an uneven paving stone: *In that instant all my discouragement disappeared and I was possessed by the same felicity which at different moments of my life had given me the view of trees which seemed familiar to me during the drive round Balbec.* Objects also help structure an argument: during a walk to "clear one's mind" an object falls out and clarifies some muddy abstract. Walking is often the encountering of the world of things, not only "out there," but for some odd reason "in here," as each step releases examples and thingamajigs—apples and wheelbarrows, plots and transitions and pi.

Altogether thinking with things is so much richer than without them. Perhaps this is why literature was for Phillip Sidney the most exalted of disciplines. Nor are poets, he argues, dependent on actual or historical things; they can create imagined worlds and imagined things:

Only the Poet disdeining to be tied to any such subjection, lifted up with the vigor of his own invention, doth grow in effect into another nature: in making things

either better then nature bringeth foorth, or quite a new, formes such as never were in nature: as the Heroes, Demigods, Cyclops, Chymeras, Furies, and such like; so as he goeth hand in hand with nature, not enclosed within the narrow warrant of her gifts, but freely raunging within the Zodiack of his owne wit.
    "The Defence of Poesie"

Exchanges with paintings or sculpture or photographs are more complicated, often lengthy, significant and unfinished. Years later, there is Manet's portrait of the woman with grapes in the Boston Museum of Fine Arts. You'd written a college paper about this painting; she comes back dragging herself and the girl you were into the room; you can see them both and your knees feel the ache of kneeling on the floor staring into another's eyes and the air of the large museum room in winter, its gloomy melancholy takes over the Santa Ana air of Los Angeles.

An Obsession with Objects

I've read that an obsession with objects is obsession for the not-that-which-I-am, the maddening bafflement that here is something I am not. Walking the world, touching whatever runs horizontally along with my hand, going along together with it until the wall runs out, the hedge stops, the ridged concrete blocks that tear the skin are no longer; one has turned left into the void. But then: there is a tree. It is a paper birch and the bark peels off in horizontal strips like paper. The papery bark is not the paper that is so often in front of me, entirely blank.

As a child I spent hours among neighborhood trees collecting twigs of various sorts and peeling off the bark until pieces were caught under my fingernails and I carried them around with me pretending to be elsewhere. That child had dirty fingernails.

Objects are so silent; they never utter anything, but just sit there rooted in the ground, sitting on the tabletop, circled around one's wrist. Keep collecting the bowls you collect and what does it get you? There they are lined up on the shelf, containers of rice for dinner on occasion, but mostly containers of air: so potent, so silent, so charged with their own being, without any concern for the comings and goings of those who pick them up, dust them off, fill and empty them. What do they remind you of; what do they ask; what history do they contain?

You touch the side of a celadon bowl. Even objects that are not containers are "emptied out," but a bowl is the purest example—the main part of the object hollow, missing. Of course children imagine themselves as containers with a hollow middle underneath the navel and they draw human families as rounded circles, the skin clearly marked by the pencil, the inside mere white paper. Perhaps these drawings already acknowledge a shared incompleteness. Negation forms part of us all thrown as we are into the world. So we continue our obsession with objects.

objecta: noun (from the verb ob+jacēre, to throw or place): a thing thrown before or presented.
Oxford English Dictionary

Visible and mobile, my body is a thing among things; it is caught in the fabric of the world, and its cohesion is that of a thing.
Maurice Merleau-Ponty

The Object in Hand

A pit opens up and as one goes under, someone's hand reaches out to hold the bedsheet. It is momentarily recognizable as one's own.

The photographer who took images of marines killed in a June 26 suicide attack and posted them on his Web site, was subsequently forbidden to work in Marine Corps-controlled areas of the country.

The inability to hook one sentence to the next seemed impossible, when the cup was passed back and forth from hand to hand and a filament of connection managed its leap through the efficacy of a conjunction.

The fruit crop is rotting, residents say, and the cost of a 66-pound bag of flour has skyrocketed to $100.

Unable to remember where the police department was located, although the route to the hardware store went directly past, and unable to recall the name of the adjacent area where the gang murder had taken place, she held to the arm of the chair, rubbing her hand back and forth on the carving.

His photos show a scene of horror with body parts littering the ground.

She found herself staring blankly at the wall as the newscaster's voice refused to dislodge itself from a low moan from behind the refrigerator in the left ear, and she put her hand to her head and held it there.

The report included the deaths of an estimated 1.7 million people through torture, execution, starvation and overwork, leaving behind a country psychologically paralyzed.

Waking early before the light had reached the room, the blurring of the various items in the room, the breathing that refused to return to normal, the frame on the bedstand falling violently to the floor, her hand having flailed against it.

The fact that these photos have been so incredibly shocking to people says that whatever they are doing to limit this type of photo getting out, it is nevertheless working.

Her meager response was to touch each object on the shelf, begging them all to remain in place, as if they could hear, as if they had motive, as if efficacious.

Collecting Air

       handmade wrap-arounds for air   enclosing emptiness
clay spun into rounded walls

spinning around air

       this merest strand as a 16th–century tune, Wyatt or Tallis,
       the voice's penumbra
       unattached extension of a shadowy note—
           sightless air, sightless   clinging

paper lifted and scudding in the vacant lot, a shoe as usual, its strap
           sticking in air

all that can't be held and
       the slippery clay spinning on the wheel

the teabowls reddish or blackened with red slip
       Chōjirō was not a myth
       one incised to order 1574   an entire exhibit of
them
a ground tea bitter to the tongue, *matcha*

       a door bangs open, shut, silence dragged away by small
instances
moving where I am moving

what I'm after is without form
       pieces rounding around it   black, pock-marked

thumbs pushing down   fingers locked in the making of absence an air on the air as the windows open

there's got to be what's missing   the precision of the
emptiness

utile, inutile,

    mixed with feldspar, mixed with water

    straight walls, a varied lip

    with translucent glaze—nothing inside

2.
PEOPLE

THE UNFAMILIAR

It seems probable that if we were never bewildered there would never be a story to tell about us; we should partake of the superior nature of the all-knowing immortals whose annals are dreadfully dull.

Henry James, *The Princess Casamassima*

It was embarrassing; it was always embarrassing, the sense of having been there before, of recognizing it all so completely—you glimpse just the back of his head several rows up, the tilt of his shoulder as he looks to the program, the overpowering way time creeps up in you through the music, so that you could walk up the aisle and sit down next to him, your skirt sticking to the backs of your knees in the humid air, the breath you allow yourself now to take, the embarrassment as he turns to his companion and turns into someone belonging only to this year and not to that other year when Webern was playing, thin, spare, almost non-existent notes, the *5 Movements for String Quartet*.

It was the not knowing the person one had lived with all those years as if the person one had had those wretched Chinese take-outs with, *Chou Chou Chinese Take Out*, the sign in neon, had been mechanically inserted into one's life the way a train is inserted in the photograph of a pastoral idyll, or the way he positioned a naked woman in a bathtub in 1988, along an abandoned road in the abandoned countryside, the muddy pool reflecting light, her legs making a V above the line of the tub, and with her face turned away so one cannot see the expression, only guess at who she might be, stuck there, as if the person you lived with all those years were simply an insert, eating moo shu pork, the man across from you, his chopsticks poised like little legs in the air.

The person most theatrical is the one you are inevitably drawn to, the one able to enter stage door left and declaim loudly despite having forgotten his lines. He is sitting at the head of the table and telling how it was when you were in Rome, how you saw the Bernini together and were together transported by the metamorphosis from marble to leaf, and how in the evenings you sipped Terre di Tufo cold from the bar and repeated the events of the day to one another as if you had actually been to the museum together, although you are certain that on that very day he had a mussed linen jacket to throw on, a conference to attend. And when he hands you the postcard you purchased, Daphne's hand reaching into the rarified air, and says he saved it for this very moment—all eyes upon him—to hand it you, to please you, you realize the lengths to which subterfuge will go and are, despite yourself, awed.

Occasionally, the drive for intimacy becomes so strong that one is willing to do anything dramatic to get it, moving beyond the usual gracious approaches, the ones viewed as most likely to produce the intimacy one seems to be seeking, to an unreasonable and even mad assault on the person and indeed the very qualities that drew you in the first place. In these instances the drive takes on a life of its own, and one finds oneself on the attack all beak and wings, plunging into the core of silence at the center of a life, fracturing the fragile threads by which connection might be formed, only to find that one has, in retaliation for its refusal to reveal itself, obliterated even the idea itself.

When he phones you can't recognize the voice in its thin greeting, its pacing and turns of phrase. And then you realize it's the voice you've overheard from the other room when you are the person slicing radishes in the kitchen and able to hand him a note reminding him to remind the person on the other end of the exact date, whereas now you are the person on the other end and have, in consequence, the same sort of unreality those others have always had for you, and so you realize that what you can't recognize isn't so much his voice and its polite inquiries, but your own position since you still imagine yourself standing in the kitchen slicing radishes, but you've been pushed out into the distance and are instead the figure, abstract and dismissible, on the other end of the phone line, and thus unable to recognize the voice that is so very familiar to you.

At that point I had traversed the room and arrived at the table at which we had thought to sit together before the events of the last few days, but which now, these events having taken place, was— even this so simple a thing—never to occur. How often one has thought: this table, these chairs, these forks and knives, and then, for reasons that afterwards one tries in vain to articulate, that particular configuration is never to be. It was imagined beforehand and can be imagined again, but then was impossible, prohibited by the emotional furor that had, one has to conclude, have overtaken and overwhelmed us. And yet, how firm the wooden top of the table, how tined the fork, and how vaporous human drama seems next to these material objects, despite its ability to alter one's relation to such objects entirely.

THE FAMILIAR

She said: someone gets under your skin, a counterpart, someone so close as to seem the one at the center of a mirror and staring back. What gets to you is this unexpectedness, its lack of category— although perhaps such a person is like the childhood friend you shared everything with, told everything to, the one you played the piano duet with and whose fingers you crossed over, whose voice you heard under the notes. She said: when she disappeared I had explanations and was given explanations by those who knew us, but they hung in the air like constructions, interesting in hypothetical ways, but disconnected, irrelevant. What I did then was dream of her as if a painting with a woman in a red dress had come alive, walked her perfume through the room and walked out again. I could understand what had happened only as something painted and framed: the woman in the Sargeant painting at the Clark, a woman wearing a gypsy skirt and a flower in her hair, Venetian glass beads looped through the fingers of her hands. A painting, she said, I've seen every summer for 25 years. Next to the painting in the museum, of course, is another painting, a quite different one. Yet, staring at the painting one has chosen, one feels—mistakenly, but surely—it has reached out and chosen you, that in the deep of the quiet halls, it stares back, and that when you walk away it has settled into your skin and erased all the other colors on the wall.

It occurs that a man who is holding a pencil may want very much to let go of it, but his hand will not let go...
     Blanchot

PORTRAITS

Rauschenberg

Can one say the stoop of her shoulder, the pull of a blouse against the back, her hair falling across her cheek? The pull of a thread at the hem, the pull of sympathy? Can one say the watering can in the Rauschenberg, the Renoir girl herself, blue pinafore, blond curls, the green watering can pasted into the collage. The whole of the past may be longed for in its wholeness, but it only reappears in such fragments, reincarnated in the stoop of her shoulder as she leans over to talk to someone. And then, although this woman is young, her stoop only a momentary break in her extraordinarily erect posture and nothing to do with the stoop of years—all that happened in black and white films she had never seen and only lately has taken to watching—has now been visited upon her by deadening images others of us know by heart.

Charcot

The leaves move outside the window of the kitchen; they do not blow, but rather from a still position move suddenly from one side to another and stop. I try to figure out how this might happen, how the wind might be caught in a particular eddy at the side of the building, how the fence just beyond might let some leak through, wind that lifts the leaves, and then hits the side of the house, stilling the branch. Standing at the stove I am frightened by the movement, the stiff green clothing of the woman. Her name is too familiar and she's come after all this time to stand at the side of the house, stare at the leaves bending and stiffening, as they take on the postures of Charcot's hysterical women. When conjoined in this way, they begin to oscillate, as if wary of whoever might be moving through the interior rooms of the house.

Henry James: "The Real Thing"

It was not so much that I recognized her with certainty, as that I was certain she was not brand new. She moved as if she were copying the ways people move. I told her that in one story the characters who were "the real thing," proved no good at playing the roles of the genteel. I always buy everything I want she said because I have no bad habits. She was addicted to buying used handbags. She arranged them along a shelf and spoke to them in their slouchy configurations as if they were dolls that would, as she remembered from childhood, come alive at night and move about. One by one, over a shoulder, by a side, clutched under an arm, they were functional enough, but lumped together on the shelf they were ciphers for the postures that seemed far more real than her own as I stared at her, certain that despite her obvious youth, I had seen her before, worn and creased and slightly used.

Lolita

She can, you realize over time, only address one person at a time in a private language whispered into an ear. Last night the film focused over and over on the adolescent's ear, the nape of her neck; she was lying by the swimming pool, her one ear exposed. She is, the woman I am speaking of—not the young girl in the film who destroys everyone's life by her seductions, advertent, inadvertent—a woman who has constructed her own language, a private language that would have been seductive many years before, but which, given her age and the use to which it has been put, is something else altogether. Yet, in the momentary thrall of such language, one experiences the days of one's adolescence when names were secrets and codes were operative—one feels the intimate violence of the voyeur.

A Lost Revelation

What she was saying to me was what I didn't want to hear her saying, which was her saying something slowly as I was racing down the stairs as I was always racing down the stairs, tripping, falling, but she was speaking to me from behind somewhere or from the further room or on the other side of the closed door I knocked before I came in where she was in the midst of the one sentence she seemed always to be in the midst of, but I was having so hard a time listening or paying attention to how slowly it was coming out of her mouth, couldn't get myself to slow my legs, kept on and on and I couldn't, although I tried, get them to stop or put one over the top of the other, hoping that might help, but the one wouldn't and the other wouldn't and I never did then hear her say what I didn't want to hear her say, although forever after I've longed to return to those stairs, that room, that knock on the door and to see myself stand there to hear what she had been saying, lost now in *the annals of time*.

Bach

The voice sings a mellow E-flat, the oboe is unforgettable in its pathos and creates the picture of one who cannot express her pain because her mouth is closed shut. The CD plays all afternoon and evening. The soprano's voice is deep and weary and won't leave me alone. The mouth that sings and the mouth that is closed have been around before in the woman whose low voice held you spellbound through all your sleepless nights so that you couldn't think to open your mouth and what did you have to say, what sorts of things could you add to the pain that wearied her and drew such circles under her eyes and what right did you have to say anything at all through those years before she vanished from sight only to reappear in Bach, *schlummert ein, ihr matten augen*.

San Nicola da Tolentino

He sits across from me even when he's not sitting across from me in a painting by Il Perugino. His eyelids are heavy, fleshy as weeds swollen with pond water. There are many ways of being original; inventing a narrative plot is only one. In the portrait the eyelids are heavy with the fatigue with which priests must look askance on the world. His face is that of someone too old for the rosy cheeks the painter's painted for him, too grave for the witty crook of fingers pointing to the Latin inscribed in the book at the center of the frame. A skeptic by nature, he has nonetheless embraced the profession, worn the black robe, sat in the arching dome across from me, called himself San Nicola da Tolentino, moved slightly to the side of the lily growing like a ragged weed behind him, the man I always see across from me.

Audubon

One summer by chance, visiting friends who had invited other friends to lunch, friends who then asked to include and did include a neighbor who was asked along, I had the opportunity to see her portfolio of road kill. The birds in her photographs were dead, their bones protruding through spread feathers held apart by disembodied hands. I asked her if she thought there was some intimate meaning to her pursuit of dead animals, dead birds, but instead of answering my question directly, she told the story of Audubon's failed efforts to paint a live bald eagle, his having to resort to killing the bird in order to be able finally to paint the picture, a picture which in the original version showed himself as artist crawling across a distant rope bridge, puny and precariously perched. In later editions of the famous book, this small self-portrait was erased.

3.
TRANSFERRED FICTIONS

A Concrete Crenellated Wall

I remember the last time I saw him, ill and vacant. A short time later he was dead. When I left, I walked to the bus stop. On my left was a government building of some sort surrounded by a wall of ridged concrete. Walking next to it, I put my left hand on the ridges and watched the fingers ripple across the concrete as I made my way forward, "out of my mind" I would have said even then. There was no way not to have reached out to whatever object the world presented to me at that moment. Given my state, nothing circumscribed my being, nothing kept it from extending outward as if in a dissolving melt. When I now walk by anything of approximately the height of that—a boxwood hedge, a stone wall around a property, a line of wooden posts—I move my hand across what seems an offered hardscape of a boxwood maze with no exit.

The New Door

The new door, she explained to him, is hardly austere enough for the barn-like structure and needs to be replaced at some future time that might, they both realized, standing at a distance for a clear view, be a time that never came or at least never came for them both. Planning becomes a grotesquely comic affair at a certain point in one's life; there are possible accidents when one is young, but later there is certainty and the choice to replace a door in the future, especially a door just installed, a grim moment of foolishness, demanding a severe bracketing of what one knows.

Yet, there they were, the excited characters in the film they watched one night, headed for Florida, closing the door on the New Jersey house they'd lived in for 30 years and opening a new one. What I remember, she said, is how flimsy the doors were in the new development by the beach, how maddeningly light reflected off the water, so blinding as to obliterate structure itself.

It's a question of not knowing since the future is never known, and yet knowing that now one's decisions are more hypothetical than ever, even such small decisions as doors. For the frontispiece to The Wings of the Dove, Henry James chose "The Doctor's Door," a photograph of a heavy wooden door surrounded by an arch of over-sized capstones. Unlike the doomed Millie it looks as if it could weather the centuries.

Where One Lives and Doesn't

The house itself is a mark of homelessness. His daughter thought that and told me over tea one day; although I don't much like tea, I like his daughter, and besides, it seemed so utterly appropriate to be drinking the imported teas of the world, teas he collects in glass jars and serves up to the, as I said, liminal and adrift. We wander in and we wander out. Although the sofas sag as if a large family of large people had sat on them or dogs bred for the ability to protect homes and hallways, they are simply elegant cast-offs, sat in by others before. The beautifully upholstered chair in Chinese silk belonged to someone's mother, but not his own, kept as a reminder of the category.

Myself, I arrived again later that season when I had finished reading another long book that had taken me several months and that then I read again because by the end I'd lost the thread, couldn't recall the beginning. The Greek woman with the German soul was waiting for him to arrive back from wherever he had gone on business, and she welcomed me and seemed glad to have someone to talk to while she did her nails. They were elegant and pale, unbitten. I didn't know women any longer, that is, after the generation of my own mother, who did such things in regular fashion at home, but she had it on a list of what to do before he came through the front door carrying the smells of ozone from the airplane or sour scents from foreign rooms. I might have been critical at some earlier time, but now I tried just to settle for the moment into whatever presented itself. The woman who presented herself to me was very thin and wore gauzy clothes that drew painful attention to this fact. Beneath the strands of her black hair, she was also beautiful.

I chatted on too intensely about the novels I was reading, novels set in foreign lands, and about my desire to return to living on the East

Coast, to the town I thought I remembered from my childhood and to streets I conflated with streets from an earlier time when I went barefoot and could feel the hot blacktop burning my feet. *I lived with him, too, you know, but of course you know,* and described a trip to a flea market at which we had bought—here I pointed—the wooden mantel that leaned in the corner, not a mantel for a fireplace or for the house itself, but as an object more beautiful because out of place and time. I spent hours removing the flecking paint from the wooden curves and indentations and photographing the process itself, enlarging portions of the scroll-like wooden corners until the resulting image resembled a pock-marked map of disproportion and confusion.

She listened to me skeptically and then told me that she thought she had worked on that mantel, but perhaps, she paused, it was on the armoire in the bedroom, a flaking and unusual piece, almost decayed, dragged in—so it seemed—from some shoreline, but a rare piece if also marred. We finished the tea. She took up again the arranging of her costume and posture, and I, ready to leave before he came through the door, felt the almost tidal pull of the pages left to read, my almost insatiable need to return to the words on a page, caught as I was in the wanderings of Lucy Snowe: *I had hoped we might reach Villette ere night set in, and that thus I might escape the deeper embarrassment which obscurity seems to throw round a first arrival at an unknown bourne; but, what with our slow progress and long stoppages—what with a thick fog and small, dense rain—darkness, that might almost be felt, had settled on the city by the time we gained its suburbs.*

Later, when I visited again, after another exhausting and round-about journey, I found that particular woman—Dimi—gone and him in the throes of arranging photographs and putting them in frames to contain them. There was little wall space left, but he rearranged and exchanged and moved a bookcase to the side, and after a day or so, I found myself looking not at Dimi but at photographs of her face enlarged to beyond life-size and filling the spot where the antique mantel had been. A new woman friend was due shortly for dinner;

she was an author or at least had been in her native country. He offered me tea, of course, something vaguely perfumed, and asked me where I'd been and at the moment he asked I couldn't remember or rather it seemed irrelevant. I couldn't think of anything but Villette whose streets I had to confess I knew better than any other, *Rue Royale*, *Rue d'Isabelle*, *Rue Villa Hermosa*, and *Rue Terarcken*.

The Pressing Machine

I was listening to the radio interview with a woman who had written a book on her own autism. I listened to the end of the program, stirring spaghetti in the pot, and waited for the anticipated moment in which I felt the symptoms, remembered, if vaguely, my own rocking, the confusion at trying to find the ground beneath as I extended my leg out of the back seat of the car and it hung in the air, posed but without purpose. The woman sounded like a good student, like one of my own students, not good at math, but good at what she called "language arts," learning early the word for *paleolithic*. As a child she had built forts out of sticks and mud behind her house. The spaghetti was muddy looking, covered in bits of chopped basil and garlic that had turned the whole the color of mortar. It was gritty under my teeth. When I woke up the room where I had fallen asleep in was still there.

The summer was wet. The pit bull was still chained up, but when I walked I carried a walking stick past the house with the fallen roof, the motor home marked with an official-looking sign, "unsafe because of gas emissions," a beagle with a deep yowl, a woman who came out occasionally to pull at a weed or two before disappearing again. The man in the yard asked if I wanted to buy a horse with one blue walleye. There's enough to think of, he said, without a horse.

Last summer I had tried not to adopt her pronunciation of "but," but the woman who said it, said it with such a seductive swing of earrings, that I couldn't help it. I imagined curling up inside the sound of the word, warm against intrusion. The woman on the radio said she just did things the way she wanted to no matter what anybody said and I believed her. This summer I found myself walking past the conversations in the garden as if they were coming as Spicer said from the radio, as if I were just picking up random static from an antenna buried in my left ear. It was John Donne who first used the work "labyrinthine" to refer to the ear. My son had wanted Q-tips but it was among the other things I'd forgotten at the store.

The store was air-conditioned an icy cold; people ran in and out rapidly leaving the aisles vacant. They ran to their cars in the rain. The small elderly woman who sounded as if she were from New York not Vermont said don't ever buy the store brand, always get Reynold's wrap can you see it dear on the shelf and would you reach it for me. My bed was a shelf under the deep eaves just like the bed I had had as a child. If I sat up too quickly I banged my head and so I had to get out carefully, sliding between the blankets and the mattress in order to leave everything flat and smooth. There was no way to stand on the other side of the bed, but I took a damp paper towel and leaned flat over the bed and mopped up the moths that had fallen during the night.

When I set out for a walk I saw a woman standing just up the road under the shade of a large tree. She stood as still as a statue, so still that it looked as if something might be the matter. It looked as if she would stare and then suddenly startle and flee back up the hill. The woman said, I'll just join you back up the hill; I never go any further; I thought my children would marry and have their children early but here I am old and they are too heavy for me to pick up. Her limp dress hung on her as if it had been made from fabric already used for something else. I began to walk as slowly as the woman. She walked slower and slower until I thought she might stop and never move again until someone else came along to prod us. I felt old as if it were contagious; that night I would dream of heavy, lumpy children.

The woman on the radio said her clothes hurt and she took off all her clothes. In order to wash my hair I lie down in the bath. There is no shower. My right knee hurts in the cramped position it needs to be in to fit into the tub and I wondered if it would always hurt or if after time it might improve. In the days of kung fu, I had often hurt my right knee kicking hard into space above the polished concrete floors, and in those days it had righted itself. But now I am not so sure. The man who mowed the lawns said that with qigong he could feel the energy moving around in his body, could drop his organs and lift them back into place.

The man who is a friend and neighbor gave repeated instructions about the code for locking the house. He was going out of town and I was to guard the house. He looked through me and saw all the pots he had collected over many years smashed by a vandal despite his precautions: all the windows were wired and the doors. The most precious pots were by the Mimbres people of the American Southwest. All the pots had been "killed" and placed over the head or face of the deceased at the time of burial, aiding the spiritual transformation of the deceased from one realm to the next. At night in the storm, heavy rain and winds, responsible for both my own cabin and the neighbor's house and pots, I thought about how in earlier years I had been afraid of being dramatically killed in the woods. I thought of myself as a person so far from anyone, so unrelated to anyone that anything could happen and no one would know. I thought about how the Mimbres poked a hole through the pot, avoiding the image of the deer, but mostly I thought about the beautiful white space on which the image had been painted.

The woman on the radio described how she likes being pressed and how her liking for being pressed influenced her invention of the pressing machine for cattle being led off to slaughter; that way, she reasoned, they wouldn't be so fearful. When I was a child I crawled between the mattress and the box springs. I asked my sister to sit on my extended legs. I crawled into the dark space behind the clothes in the closet so I didn't have to see anyone, not even myself. In the back of my cabin the cows make a sound that is clearly distinct, but sounds like the machines mowing hay in the distance.

Posada

For seventeen years I practiced kung fu. I wasn't young when I started and I stopped when the fear of falling and cracking my bones on the waxed concrete floor in slippery kung fu slippers came to be real rather than an abstract idea, and because of something else.

The best student in the advanced class, a man who had come for years and whom we all looked to as a model for our own punches and kicks, gave up waiting to be given the mantle and left. He'd come to the evening class at the same time for years and years; one day without saying anything to anyone, he stopped. We all whispered to one another in the changing room. He should have been told the studio would be passed to him; he should have been singled out in some way. But he wasn't. Had he simply left in anger, disappointment, or had he learned what he had come to learn? The master kept silent.

That winter our 72-year-old Chinese master lost his voice to bronchitis and put the warm-up instructions on tape. After his voice returned, they stayed on tape, and we all saw in this a lesson in being able to learn without his presence. We were always finding lessons in his smallest decisions or gestures, no matter how eccentric. He didn't come out of his office until the final part of the class in which we practiced forms and even then he refused to speak up and correct us. This was, we assured ourselves, to make us all the more independent, to prepare us for the future. We were, he said, preparing for a battle thirty years hence.

When I first began I went to class three times a week, later two. I didn't know why I continued for so long, what I was clinging to, but I did know why I began. My mother was dying and I was helpless. She lived far away on an island off the coast of Florida, and although

I went as often as I could as a working single mother, I couldn't be there often enough. She grew thinner and thinner; her head was bald, her skin translucent. The shots of morphine didn't help.

I had first seen José Guadalupe Posada's work that year: skeletons on horseback, lances held high in the air, a battle between bones. I bought postcards of his skeletons and tacked them above my desk. I decided that although I would lose the battle with death, I would at least do battle and I signed up for kung fu. With a somewhat hysterical love, I loved the exact routinized movements, the same set of warm-ups, the same sets of punches and kicks, the same forms. I fell into the routine as if I could stop time, giving myself over to exhaustion for the hour in which I was unable to think or feel anything except the bottoms of my feet through the thin kung fu shoes, my own sore muscles, my concentration on how to perfect a move, my ingrained effort not to disappoint. I had met a woman from Hong Kong who, it seemed to me in a moment of insight or identification, wanted to stop time. I could see how she contrived and failed to do it; kung fu was my way, I now think: repetition and more repetition and the mindlessness that comes with a physical address to the world. I needed to be taken over. For the hour in class, time had no meaning.

What is harder for me to understand is why after my mother's death I kept on; and why for years after that. The year of my mother's dying unleashed a multitude of fears.

Of death, obviously. But I was also, I think now as I think back on those seventeen years, fearful of failure, fearful of what would happen to my son, fearful of being alone, fearful of the narrow-faced men on the road who called out after me, and fearful of my own sexual impulses that seemed ever to be taking me in directions I didn't want to go, that lurked even when I hid out from them. For several hours a week I was relieved of this welling up by sheer physical exertion and exhaustion.

I was in a class of almost all men and was trying to do what most of my colleagues and friends would have thought, if they had known, quite strange. Who was that person, I ask now, who liked putting on baggy cotton trousers and kung fu t-shirts, slippers impregnated with wax? Who was that person who drove through the dark to the wooden box of a studio in order to imagine herself a skeletal warrior? Because of the class, I came to know who people were not through conversation, but by how they moved, how they were tall or short, whose legs and arms I wanted to imitate, how when Sifu put his hand on his gray beard and stroked it, I was willing to try the impossible. I came to know something about the importance and reassurance of the physical world. I think I came to see a bit more of how people stood not only how they said they stood. I had lost the battle I had come to fight long before I left the class.

Yet I kept going for seventeen more years and then, as I said, I stopped—something about increased uncertainty, the slippery floor, my own aging body, the fact of bad traffic making the drive to the studio in Hollywood twice as long. But I stopped not only because of uncertainty as threat; I stopped also because I came to understand uncertainty as linked to the change that time brings. The class had allowed me to imagine I could stop time and fend off fear; now it allowed me to understand, with effort and after many years, that I could not. It was time to stop and so I did.

Bibliography

Adam Fuss. Edited by Thomas Kellein. New York: Distributed Art Publishers, 2003.

Adam Fuss. Essay by Eugenia Parry. Santa Fe, NM: Arena Editions, 2000.

Baudelaire, Charles-Pierre. "A Philosophy of Toys." In *The Painter of Modern Life and Other Essays*. Translated by Jonathan Mayne. London: Phaidon Press, 1964.

Benjamin, Walter. "The Sock" and "Unpacking My Library: A Talk about Book Collecting." In *Berlin Childhood around 1900*. Cambridge, MA: Belknap Press, 2006.

Blanchot, Maurice. *The Station Hill Blanchot Reader*. Edited by George Quasha. Translated by Lydia David, Paul Auster, and Robert Lamberton. Barrytown, NY: Station Hill Press, 1999.

Bogardus, Ralph. *Pictures and Texts: Henry James, A.L. Coburn, and New Ways of Seeing in Literary Culture*. Ann Arbor, MI: UMI Research Press, 1984.

Brown, Bill. *A Sense of Things: The Object Matter of American Literature*. Chicago: University of Chicago Press, 2003.

Cather, Willa. *The Professor's House*. Radford, VA: Wilder Publications, 2008.

Fuss, Adam. *My Ghost*. Santa Fe, NM: Twin Palms Publishers, 2002.

George Eastman House Still Photograph Archive. "Man Ray: 12 Rayographs." http://www.geh.org/amico2000/htmlsrc/index.html.

Gross, Kenneth. *Puppet: An Essay on Uncanny Life*. Chicago: University of Chicago Press, 2011.

In Focus: László Moholy-Nagy. Los Angeles: The J. Paul Getty Museum, 1995.

Jacobs, Karen, ed. "Photography and Literature." Special issue, *English Language Notes*, 44.2 (Fall–Winter 2006).

James, Henry. *The American Scene*.

———*The Golden Bowl*.

———"The Real Thing."

———*The Princess Casamassima*.

———*The Sacred Fount*.

———*The Spoils of Poynton*.

———*The Wings of the Dove*.

Johnson, Barbara. *Persons and Things*. Cambridge, MA: Harvard University Press, 2008.

Krauss, Rosalind. "The Photographic Conditions of Surrealism." In *The Originality of the Avant-Garde and Other Modernist Myths*. Cambridge, MA: MIT Press, 1985.

Moholy-Nagy, László. *Painting Photography Film*. Cambridge, MA: MIT Press, 1967.

Neruda, Pablo. *Odes to Common Things*. Selected and illustrated by Ferris Cook. Translated by Ken Krabbenhoft. Boston, MA: Bullfinch Press, 1994.

Neusüss, Floris M., Thomas F. Barrow, and Charles Hagen. *Experimental Vision: The Evolution of the Photogram since 1919*. Boulder, CO: Robert Rhinehart Publishers, 1994.

Perec, Georges. *Species of Spaces and Other Places*.

Ponge, Francis. *The Voice of Things*.

Rudnick, Les. "The Photogram—A History: Captured Shadows; The Shadows That Things Make, the Things That Shadows Make." http://www.photograms.org/chapter01.html.

Schwenger, Peter. *The Tears of Things: Melancholy and Physical Objects*. Minneapolis, MN: University of Minnesota Press, 2006.

Welling, James. *James Welling: Flowers*. New York: David Zwirner, 2007.

Woolf, Virginia. "Solid Objects." In *A Haunted House and Other Short Stories*. http://www.photograms.org/introduction.hml.

Acknowledgements

"The Pressing Machine" ("Things in Vermont"), *Seneca Review*, spring 2006.

"One summer by chance," "The voice sings a mellow E-flat," "The leaves move outside the window," *Interim*, Vol. 26 #1&2, 2008.

"Is intimacy held tight in the gesture," *Pleiades*, 29.1.

"You enter a room in which each item has been carefully placed," "Looking at the folded muslin," "The seashell disintegrates into your hand," "The cup on the shelf above eyelevel," "One turns against oneself at the thought" *Web Conjunctions*, 2008.

"If the photograph itself is of objects in a shop window," "The book lies open and prone," "No one else seems to catch the overwhelming odor," *Burnside Review*, Vol. 4 #1.

"Can one say the stoop of her shoulder," "The leaves move outside the window," "It was not so much that I recognized her with certainty," "The voice sings a mellow E-flat," *chapbook* for a reading at Bergamot Station, ed. Susan Sizor 2008.

"The word in the sentence has been smudged," "For a writer, the intimacy of the image," "What difference does it make that the object in question," "Intimacy in its purest form," *OR #1*, October 2008.

"The Theater," "a photographic album," "the book," "a portfolio," "the leaves," *Boston Review*, January/February 2009.

"Rauschenberg," "Audubon," "Bach," "A silhouette," *Denver Quarterly*, spring 2009.

"Li Po," "Lolita," "Henry James: The Real Thing," *Colorado Review*, fall 2009.

"The paperclip," "L'objet entre le papier," "Against deep black the crook," *OR #3*. 2009.

"Where one lives and doesn't," *NOON #10* (titled: "He's a Prey to such women"), 2010.

"Corroded metal," "The Window," "A postcard photograph," *Denver Quarterly*, spring 2010.

"An Obsession with Objects," *Poets on Teaching*, ed. Joshua Marie Wilkinson, University of Iowa Press, 2010.

"It is useful to sit on if you're small," "What difference does it make that the object in question," *Sentence #9*, ed. Richard Deming, 2011.

Martha Ronk is the author of nine books of poetry, including *Partially Kept*, (Nightboat Books), *Vertigo* (Coffee House), a National Poetry Series Selection, *In a landscape of having to repeat* (Omnidawn), a PEN/USA best poetry book 2005, and *Why/Why Not* (University of California Press). She has also published a fictional memoir, *Displeasures of the Table*, and a collection of fiction, *Glass Grapes and other stories* (BOA Editions 2008); her poetry is included in the anthologies *Lyric Postmodernisms* (Counterpath Press), *American Hybrid*, (Norton), and *Not For Mothers Only* (Fence). She had residencies at Djerassi and The MacDowell Colony, and taught summer programs at the University of Colorado and Naropa; in 2007 she received an NEA Award. She worked as editor for Littoral Books and *The New Review of Literature*, and is the Irma and Jay Price Professor of English at Occidental College in Los Angeles, teaching Renaissance Literature and Creative Writing.

Transfer of Qualities
by Martha Ronk

Cover text set in Hypatia Sans Pro.
Interior text set in Joanna MT Std, Goudy Oldstyle Std,
and Hypatia Sans Pro.

Cover art by Farrah Karepetian
Untitled (Broken Jelly Jar, Spacious), 2007
Unique silver gelatin photogram 12.1 x 11.1 x 28.3 cm
From the collection of Kristin Rey and Michael Rubel

Cover and interior design by Cassandra Smith

Omnidawn Publishing
Richmond, California
2013

Rusty Morrison & Ken Keegan, Senior Editors & Publishers
Cassandra Smith, Poetry Editor & Book Designer
Gillian Hamel, Poetry Editor & OmniVerse Managing Editor
Sara Mumolo, Poetry Editor
Peter Burghardt, Poetry Editor & Book Designer
Turner Canty, Poetry Editor
Liza Flum, Poetry Editor & Social Media
Sharon Osmond, Poetry Editor & Bookstore Outreach
Juliana Paslay, Fiction Editor & Bookstore Outreach Manager
Gail Aronson, Fiction Editor
RJ Ingram, Social Media
Pepper Luboff, Feature Writer
Craig Santos Perez, Media Consultant